XTREME UNIVERSE

GALAXIES

AND MORE GIANT MARVELS

A&D Xtreme
BOLD HI-LO NONFICTION
An imprint of Abdo Publishing
abdobooks.com

ANN WILLIAMS

TAKE IT TO THE XTREME!

GET READY FOR AN EXTREME ADVENTURE! THE PAGES OF THIS BOOK WILL TAKE YOU INTO THE THRILLING WORLD OF ASTRONOMICAL WONDERS. WHEN YOU HAVE FINISHED READING THIS BOOK, TAKE THE XTREME CHALLENGE ON PAGE 45 ABOUT WHAT YOU'VE LEARNED!

ABDOBOOKS.COM
Published by Abdo Publishing, a division of ABDO, PO Box 398166, Minneapolis, Minnesota 55439.

Printed in the United States of America, North Mankato, MN.
102024
012025

Design: Kelly Doudna, Mighty Media, Inc.
Production: Mighty Media, Inc.
Editor: Katherine Chu

Cover Photograph: NASA/JPL-Caltech
Interior Photographs: aiva./Flickr, p. 12; CSIRO/Shaun Amy, pp. 18–19; ESA/NASA/JPL-Caltech/NHSC, p. 44; ESO/Digitized Sky Survey 2, pp. 32–33; ESO VLT MUSE/Wikimedia Commons, pp. 38–39; Grote Reber, edited by Zukaz/Wikimedia Commons, p. 16; Grote Reber/Wikimedia Commons, p. 17; Henry-Julien Detouche/Wikimedia Commons, pp. 12–13; The International Astronomical Union/Martin Kornmesser, pp. 28–29; Juliancolton/Wikimedia Commons, pp. 10–11; Martijn Oei/Wikimedia Commons, pp. 22–23; NASA, pp. 14–15, 42–43; NASA/Damian Peach, Amateur Astronomer, pp. 34–35; NASA/JPL-Caltech, pp. 1, 8–9; NASA/JPL-Caltech/ESA/Harvard-Smithsonian CfA, pp. 4–5; NASA, ESA, CXC, C. Ma, H. Ebeling and E. Barrett (University of Hawaii/IfA), et al. and STScI, pp. 24–25; NASA/JPL-Caltech/T. Pyle (SSC), pp. 26–27; NASA/JPL-Caltech/VLA/MPIA, pp. 6–7; NASA/Marshall Space Flight Center, pp. 40–41; NASA/SDO (AIA), pp. 30–31; NRAO/AUI/NSF, pp. 20–21; Space Telescope Science Institute Office of Public Outreach/NASA, ESA, CSA, STScI, Klaus Pontoppidan (STScI), p. 38; Wikimedia Commons, pp. 36–37
Design Elements: Arafat/Adobe Stock (header background); pixel/Adobe Stock (universe); Sergey Nivens/Shutterstock Images (header background)

LIBRARY OF CONGRESS CONTROL NUMBER: 2024938306
PUBLISHER'S CATALOGING-IN-PUBLICATION DATA
Names: Williams, Ann, author.
Title: Galaxies and more giant marvels / by Ann Williams
Description: Minneapolis, Minnesota : ABDO Publishing, 2025 | Series: Xtreme universe | Includes online resources and index.
Identifiers: ISBN 9781098295059 (lib. bdg.) | ISBN 9798384915102 (ebook)
Subjects: LCSH: Galaxies--Juvenile literature. | Solar system--Juvenile literature. | Universe--Juvenile literature. | Outer space--Exploration--Juvenile literature. | Astronomy--Juvenile literature.
Classification: DDC 523.112--dc23

CONTENTS

HUGER THAN HUGE 4

WHAT IS A GALAXY? 6

OBSERVING GALAXIES 10

RADIO ASTRONOMY 16

GIGANTIC GALAXIES 22

STAR SYSTEMS 26

HUMONGOUS STARS 30

ENORMOUS PLANETS 34

HUGE AND HUMANMADE 40

GREAT SPACE WONDERS 44

XTREME CHALLENGE 45

GLOSSARY 46

ONLINE RESOURCES 47

INDEX 48

CHAPTER 1

HUGER THAN HUGE

The universe is vast and filled with many huge things. If you think a planet is gigantic, a star is bigger. A star system is even bigger than a star, and a galaxy is larger than a star system. Galaxies are some of the biggest things in the universe!

The Messier 81 galaxy is located in the same constellation as the Big Dipper.

CHAPTER 2

WHAT IS A GALAXY?

A galaxy is a very large group of rocks, planets, stars, and star systems. These elements are all held together by gravity. A galaxy can be more than 100,000 light-years across.

XTREME FACT

Scientists measure size and distance in space in light-years. A light-year is the distance light travels in one year. One light-year equals about 5.88 trillion miles (9.46 trillion km).

The Southern Pinwheel galaxy, or M83. A galaxy can have billions of stars and star systems.

The Milky Way is a spiral galaxy.

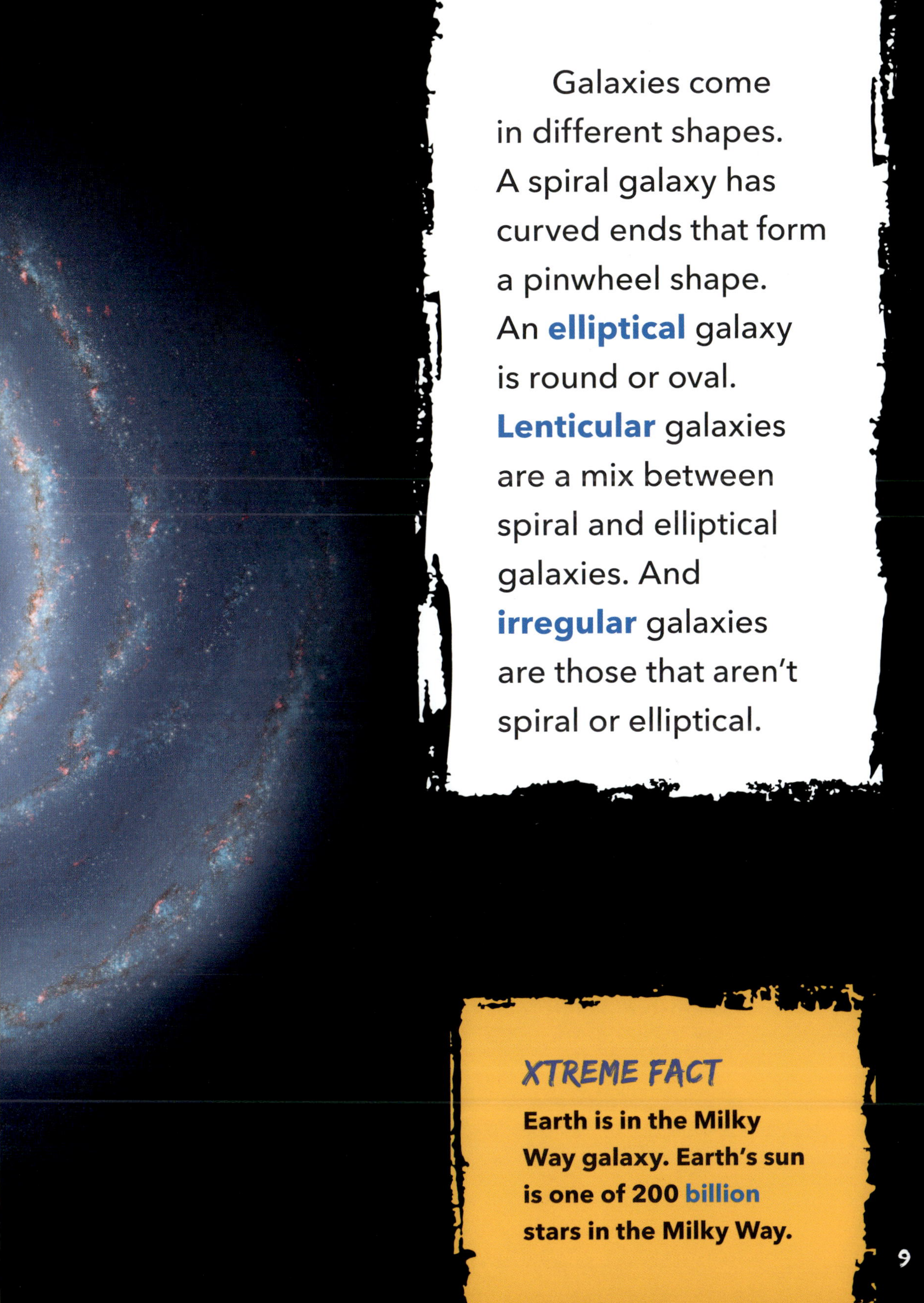

Galaxies come in different shapes. A spiral galaxy has curved ends that form a pinwheel shape. An **elliptical** galaxy is round or oval. **Lenticular** galaxies are a mix between spiral and elliptical galaxies. And **irregular** galaxies are those that aren't spiral or elliptical.

XTREME FACT

Earth is in the Milky Way galaxy. Earth's sun is one of 200 billion stars in the Milky Way.

CHAPTER 3

OBSERVING GALAXIES

The Milky Way has different names in different cultures. For example, in China it is called the Silver River. And in southern Africa, it is called the Backbone of Night.

The first galaxy observed by humans was the Milky Way. From Earth, the Milky Way looks like a curved white **streak**. According to an ancient Greek myth, the goddess Hera created the Milky Way. She sprayed milk across the sky. This is where the name Milky Way comes from.

Many ancient astronomers believed stars made up the Milky Way. But they didn't have the tools to see it clearly. This changed in the 1600s when the telescope was invented.

Italian astronomer Galileo Galilei was one of the first to study the Milky Way with a telescope. He confirmed that it was made up of thousands of stars.

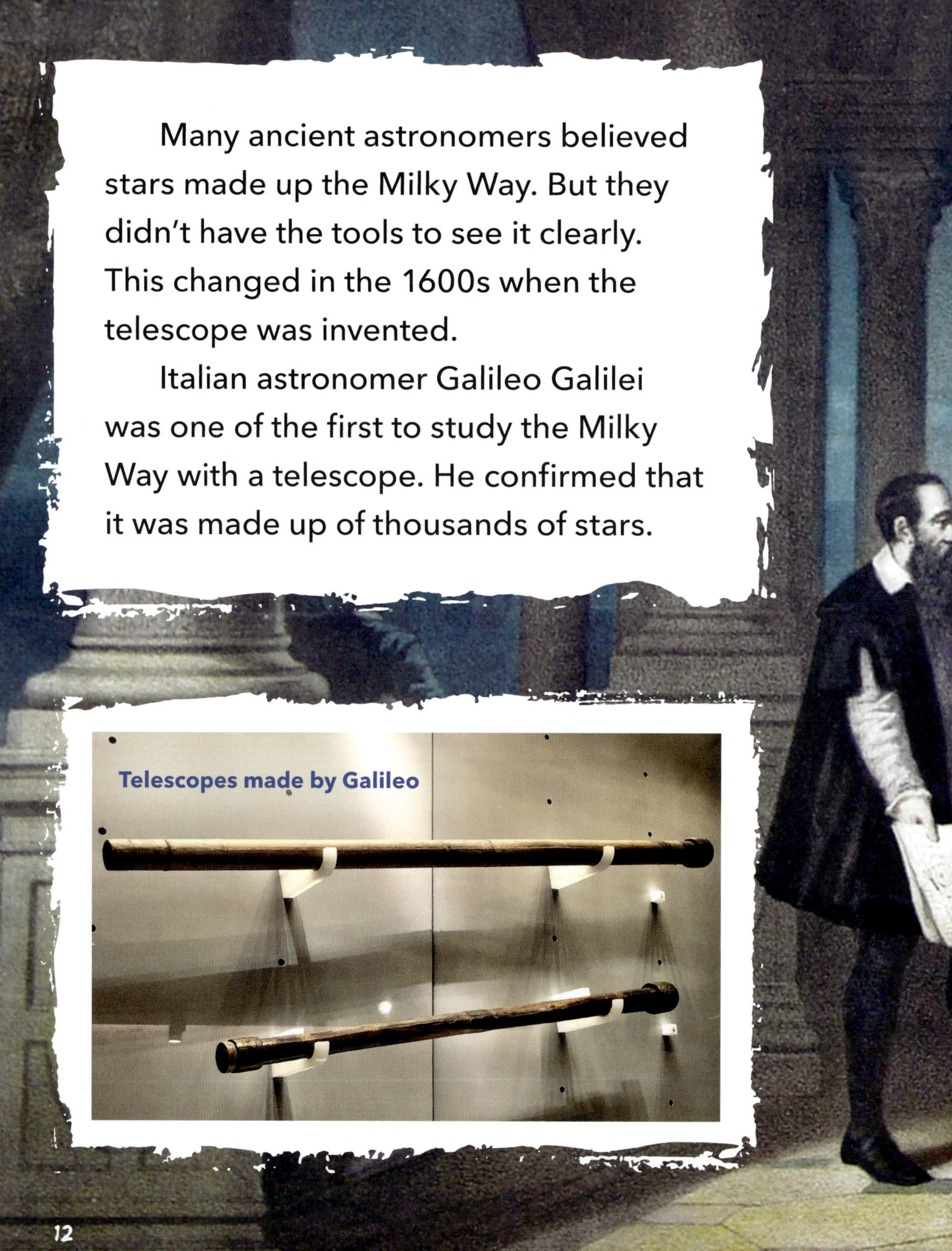

Telescopes made by Galileo

Galileo (*left*) made his own telescope after hearing about its creation in the Netherlands. He worked to improve his telescopes, making them so powerful, he could see into space.

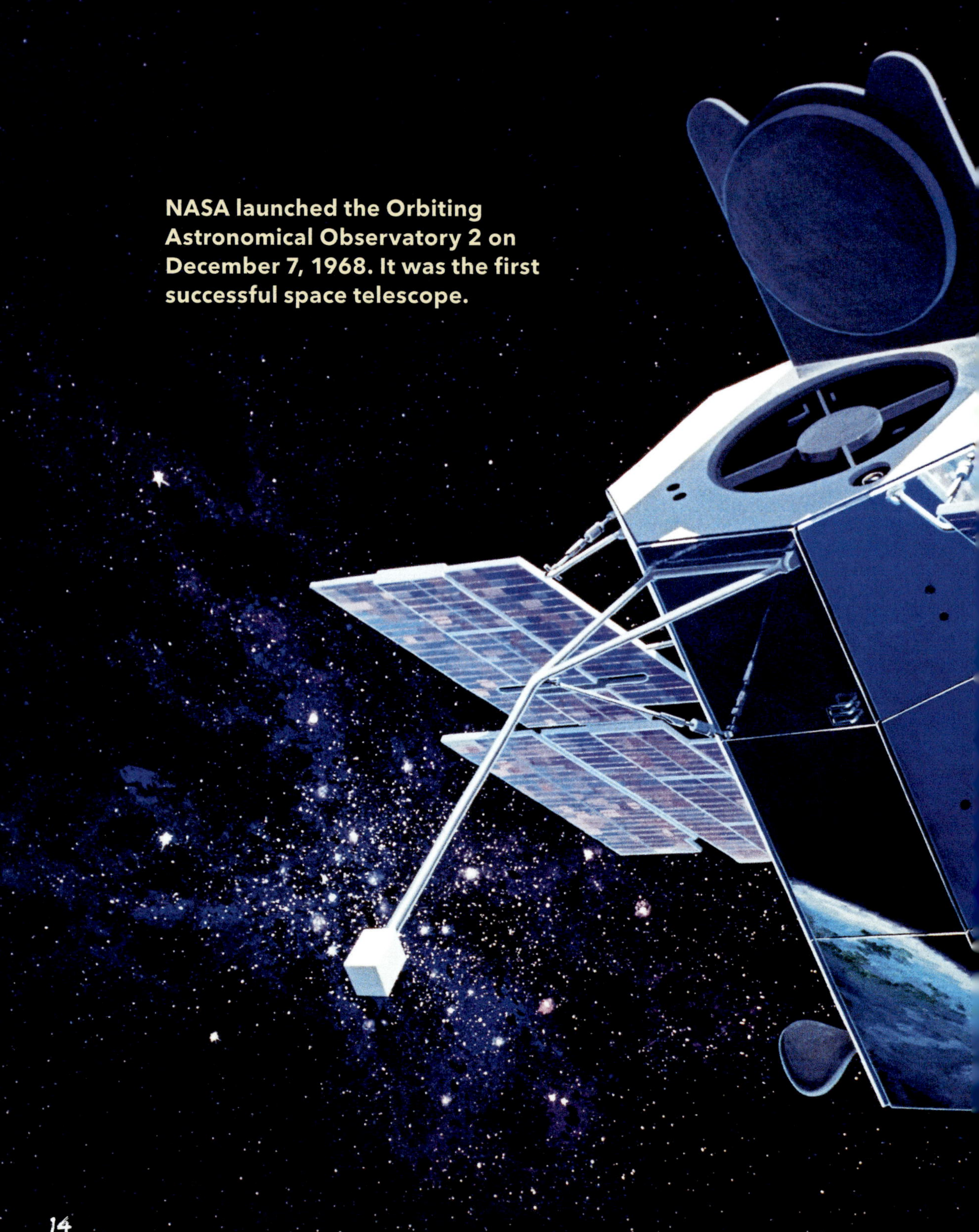

NASA launched the Orbiting Astronomical Observatory 2 on December 7, 1968. It was the first successful space telescope.

As telescopes improved, scientists could see even farther into space. They discovered galaxies beyond the Milky Way.

In 1968, the first telescope was **launched** into space. There are currently more than 20 active space telescopes. They send photos and other information back to scientists on Earth.

CHAPTER 4

RADIO ASTRONOMY

Regular telescopes use light to create visual images. But they aren't the only way scientists observe space. In 1932, engineer Karl Guthe Jansky worked at Bell Laboratories in New Jersey. He wanted to know why **static** interfered with long-distance radio communication. He found that the static was caused by radio waves coming from outside Earth's star system. Jansky's discovery led to the science of radio astronomy.

In 1944, astronomer Grote Reber created the first radio map of the Milky Way.

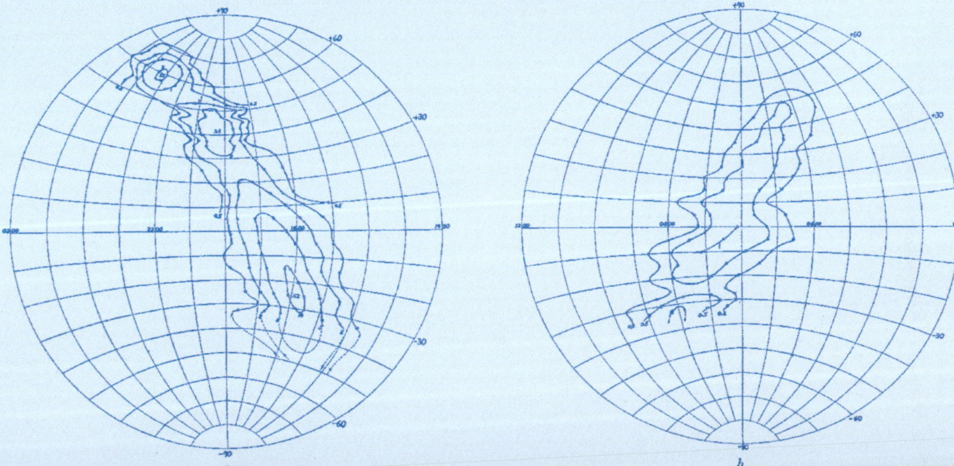

Reber invented the first radio telescope with a dish in 1937.

Radio astronomers use radio telescopes to study galaxies and other space objects. These telescopes have an antenna and a receiver that detect radio waves in space. The information is sent to a computer, which creates an image of the object that **emitted** the radio waves.

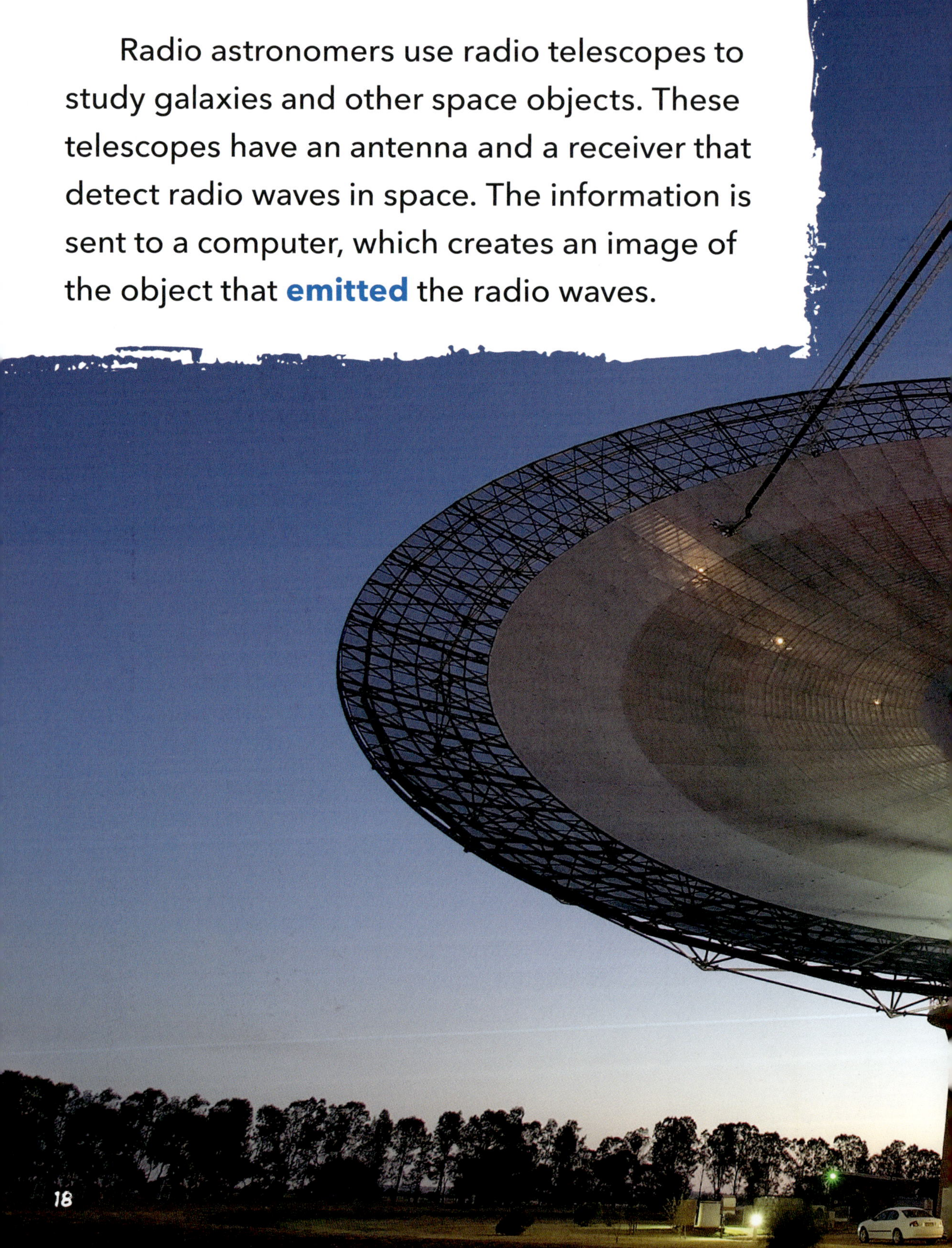

The Parkes Observatory radio telescope in Australia. Many radio telescope antennas have a large dish. Radio waves bounce off this dish and into the antenna's tip.

The Karl G. Jansky Very Large Array in New Mexico has 28 radio telescopes.

Sometimes, multiple radio antennas are connected to one another. They form a radio telescope **array**. An array can receive more information from farther away than a single radio telescope can. This creates a clearer image of different space objects.

CHAPTER 5

GIGANTIC GALAXIES

All galaxies are **extremely** large, but some are larger than others. In 2022, Dutch astronomers discovered a new galaxy. They called it Alcyoneus. It is one of the biggest known galaxies.

XTREME FACT

Most galaxies have black holes at their centers. A black hole is an area where the gravity is so strong that everything nearby gets sucked into it. Not even light can escape a black hole's gravity!

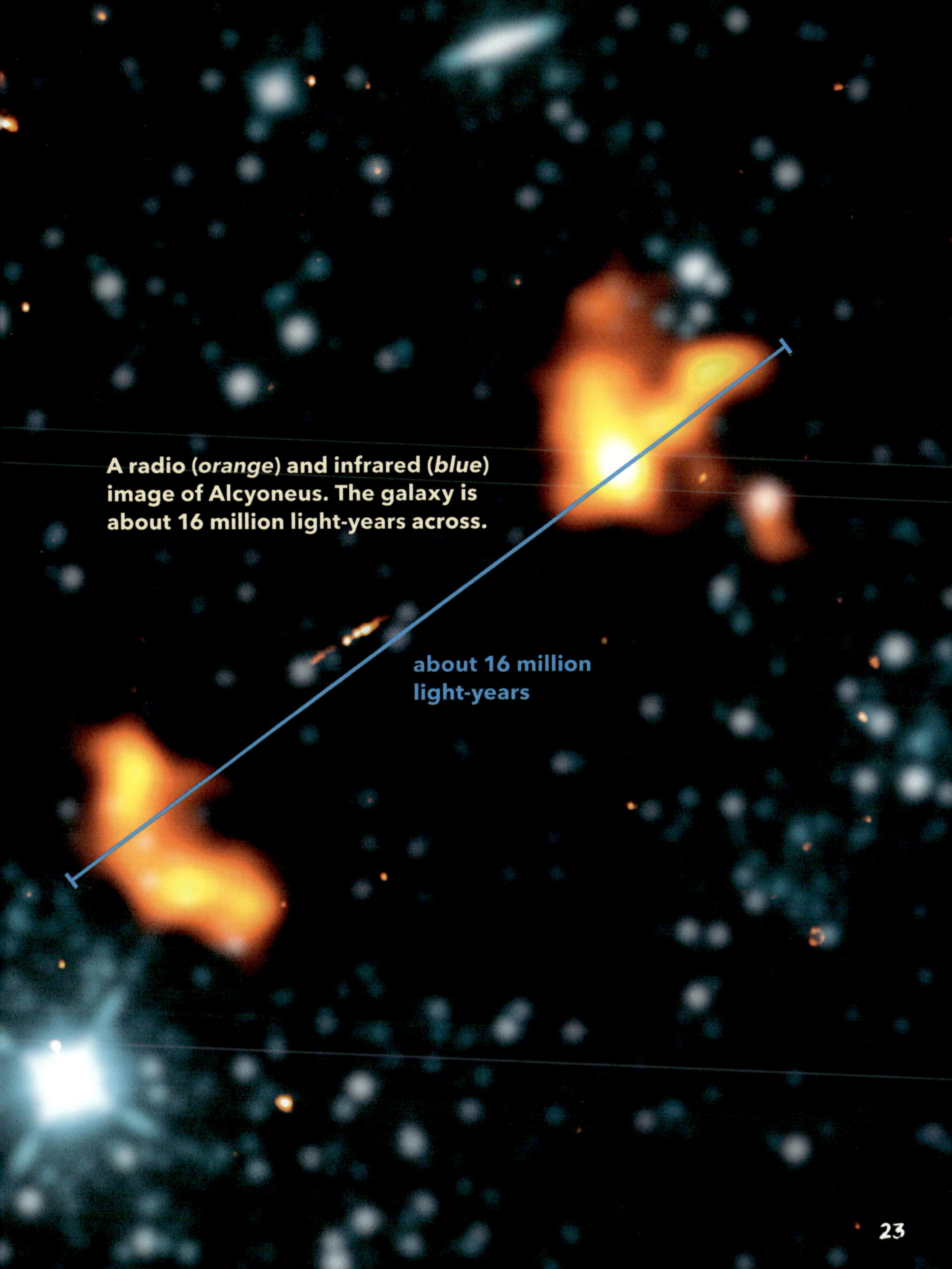

A radio (*orange*) and infrared (*blue*) image of Alcyoneus. The galaxy is about 16 million light-years across.

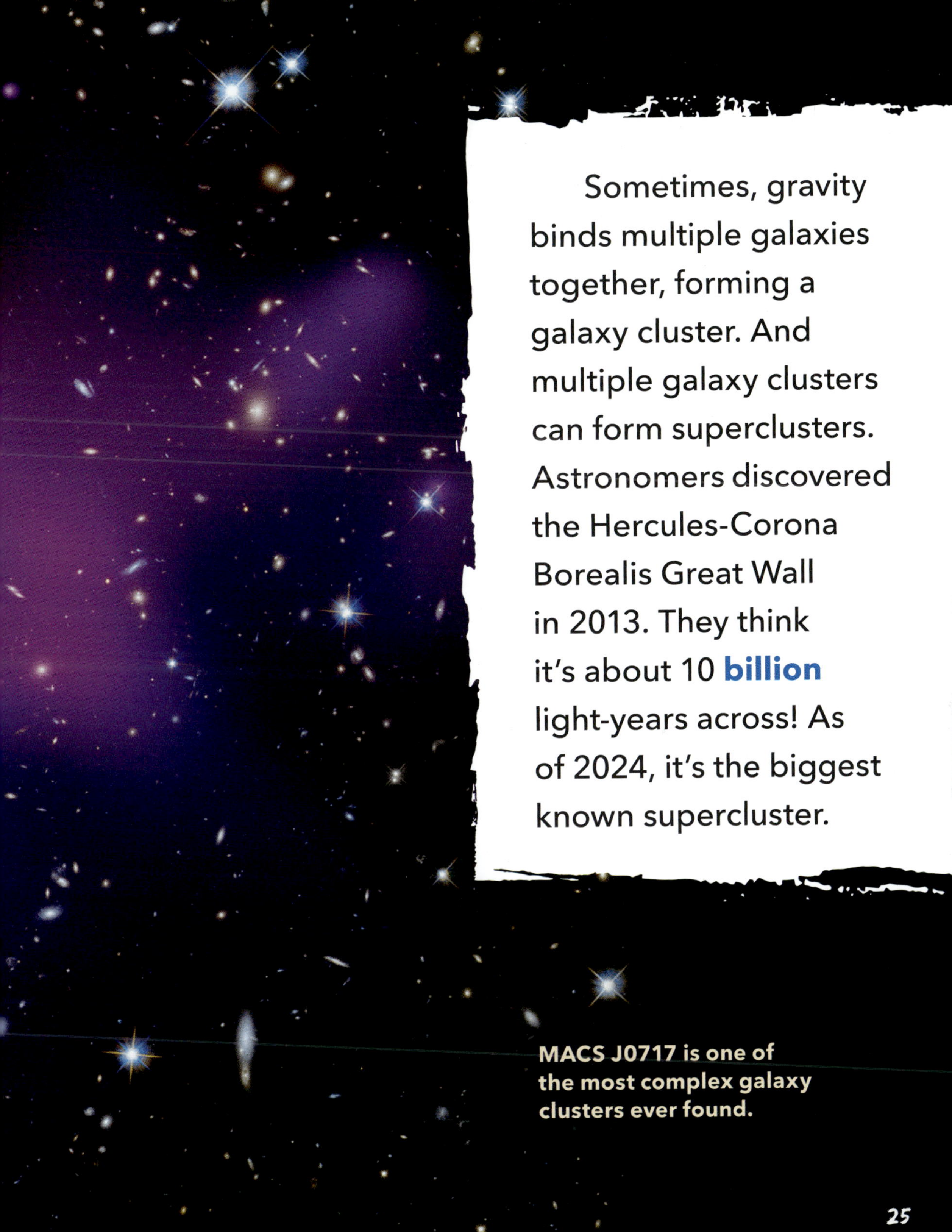

Sometimes, gravity binds multiple galaxies together, forming a galaxy cluster. And multiple galaxy clusters can form superclusters. Astronomers discovered the Hercules-Corona Borealis Great Wall in 2013. They think it's about 10 **billion** light-years across! As of 2024, it's the biggest known supercluster.

MACS J0717 is one of the most complex galaxy clusters ever found.

CHAPTER 6

STAR SYSTEMS

Galaxies are immense and made up of other **extremely** large things. These include star systems. A star system is a large star orbited by planets, moons, and other space objects. The star's gravity keeps these objects in its orbit.

Some star systems have multiple large stars that orbit each other. HD 98800 is a quadruple star system. It has two pairs of stars that orbit each other.

The Earth's star system is called the solar system. And the sun is the star in the center of the solar system. The solar system is about two light-years across. Earth and seven other planets orbit the sun. The solar system also includes many dwarf planets, moons, asteroids, and **comets**.

The Earth's star system is called the solar system because *Sol* is the Latin name for the sun.

CHAPTER 7

HUMONGOUS STARS

The biggest object in a star system is the star at the center of it. The sun is about 865,000 miles (1.4 million km) across. It's made of several gases. The most common gases in the sun are **hydrogen** and **helium**. The sun's strong gravity holds the gases together, creating a ball shape.

About 1.3 million Earths could fit inside the sun!

There are different kinds of stars. The types are based on size and heat. The sun is a yellow dwarf star. As big as it is, the sun is considered a medium-sized star.

The biggest known star is a red **hypergiant** star called UY Scuti. It is about 738 million miles (1.2 **billion** km) across.

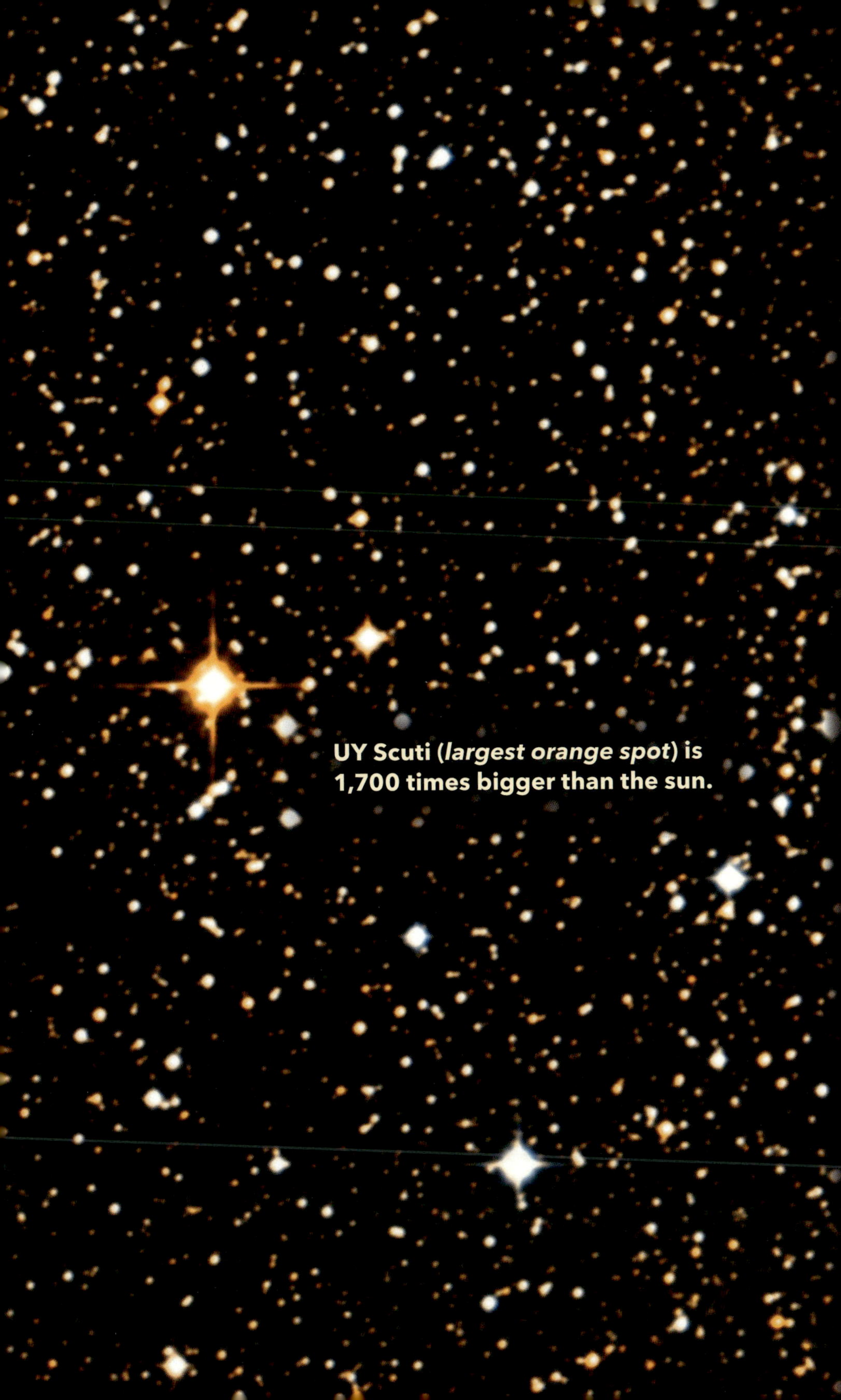

UY Scuti (*largest orange spot*) is 1,700 times bigger than the sun.

CHAPTER 8

ENORMOUS PLANETS

The biggest objects orbiting a star in a star system are usually planets. Jupiter is the largest planet in the solar system. It is about 89,000 miles (143,000 km) across. Jupiter is called a gas giant. This means it doesn't have a solid surface. Instead, it is made up of gases.

XTREME FACT

Jupiter has nearly 100 moons!

Jupiter is big enough to hold more than 1,000 Earths.

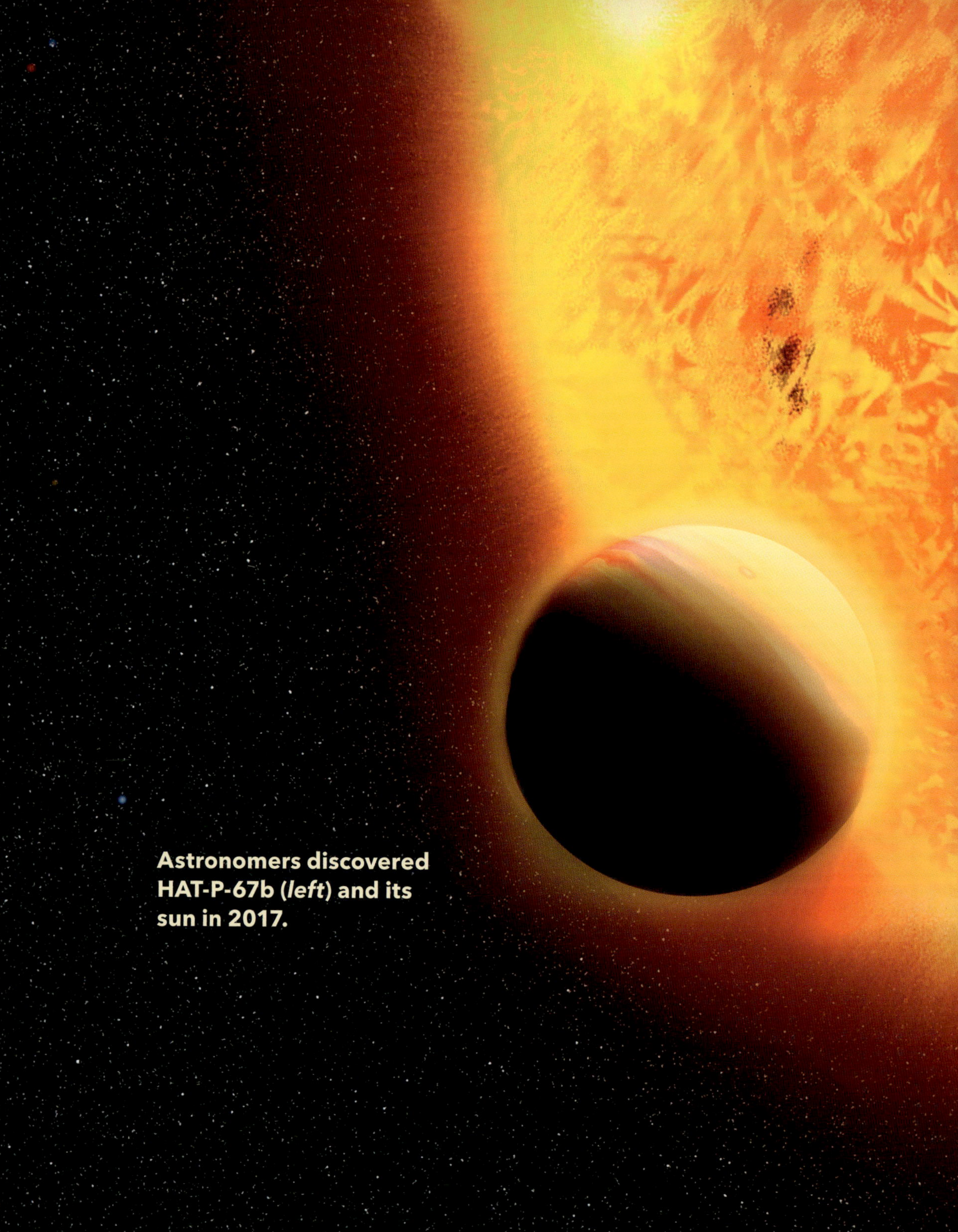

Astronomers discovered HAT-P-67b (*left*) and its sun in 2017.

There are planets even bigger than Jupiter outside our solar system. Scientists measure planets by size and mass. One of the largest planets by size is a gas giant called HAT-P-67b. It is 1,200 light-years from Earth and about twice as big as Jupiter.

Often, the bigger a planet is, the higher its mass will be. But that is not always the case. For example, HAT-P-67b is bigger than Jupiter in size, but its mass is lower than Jupiter's.

Another enormous planet is ROXs 42 B b. It is about 460 light-years from Earth and about twice the size of Jupiter. However, ROXs 42 B b's mass is about nine times greater than Jupiter's.

ROXs 42 B b (*inset*) was discovered in 2013. It is located in the Rho Ophiuchi cloud complex (*background*).

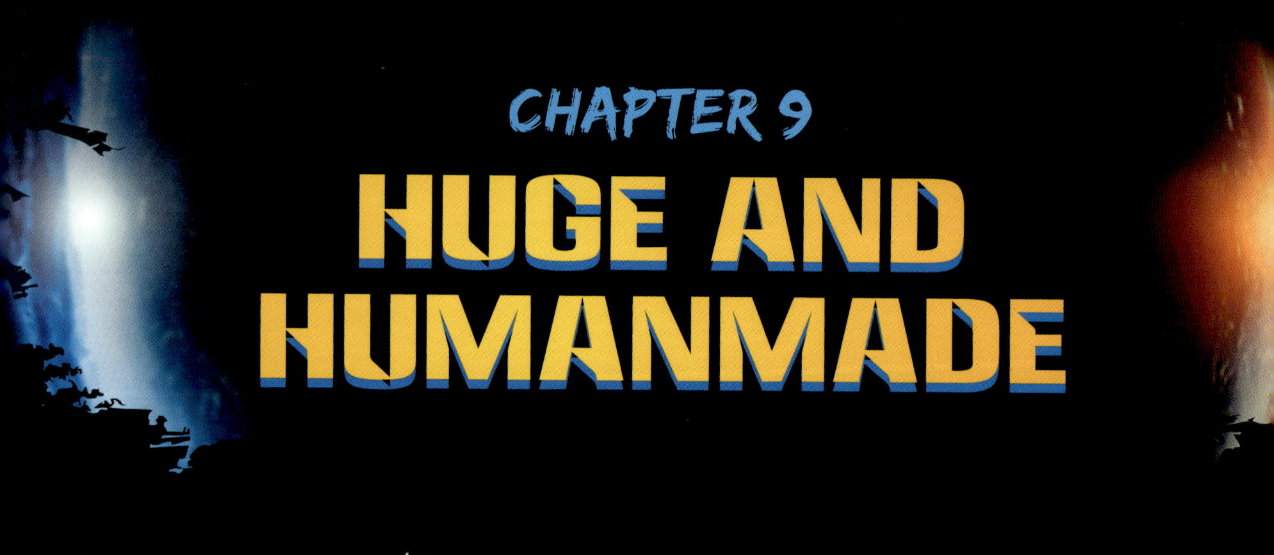

CHAPTER 9
HUGE AND HUMANMADE

Natural space objects aren't the only things in space. Since the 1950s, humans have **launched** hundreds of artificial objects into space. These include rockets, rovers, **satellites**, telescopes, and more. The biggest artificial space object is the International Space Station (ISS). It was launched in November 1998.

Scientists from 5 space agencies and 15 countries worked together to build the ISS.

The ISS is 357 feet (108 m) long. This is about as long as a football field! Astronauts live and work on the ISS. While there, they perform scientific experiments. They also maintain the ISS, repairing things when necessary.

Astronauts Loral O'Hara (*above*) and Jasmin Moghbeli (*right*) working on the ISS on November 1, 2023.

XTREME FACT

Astronauts usually spend about six months on the ISS. But from 2015 to 2016, American astronaut Scott Kelly was on board for 340 days!

CHAPTER 10

GREAT SPACE WONDERS

Galaxies, stars, and planets are some of the biggest things in the universe. Scientists continue to look farther into space to find new galaxies. They study galaxies and the objects in them to learn more about the universe and how it formed.

The Andromeda galaxy (*pictured*) is the closest giant galaxy to the Milky Way.

XTREME CHALLENGE

TAKE THE QUIZ BELOW AND PUT WHAT YOU'VE LEARNED TO THE TEST!

1) What is a galaxy?
2) What type of galaxy is the Milky Way?
3) Who is known for discovering radio waves coming from space?
4) What are the two main gases in the sun?
5) If you went to the ISS, what would you want to do there?

GLOSSARY

array–a large number or group.

billion–the number 1,000,000,000, or one thousand million.

comet–a mass of ice and dust that moves through space and develops a tail as it nears the sun.

elliptical–having an oval or circle shape.

emit–to give off or out.

extremely–to a degree that exceeds the ordinary or expected.

helium–a light, colorless gas that does not burn.

hydrogen–a gas with no smell or color that is lighter than air and catches fire easily.

hypergiant–a very massive and bright star.

irregular–not evenly or uniformly shaped, arranged, or spaced.

launch–to send a spacecraft into space.

lenticular–curved on both sides, similar to a lentil.

satellite–a manufactured object that orbits and relays scientific information back to Earth.

static–electrical discharges in the air that interfere with radio or television signals and cause a hissing, crackling sound.

streak–a long, thin mark or stripe.

trillion–the number 1,000,000,000,000, or one thousand billion.

ONLINE RESOURCES

To learn more about galaxies, please visit **abdobooklinks.com** or scan this QR code. These links are routinely monitored and updated to provide the most current information available.

INDEX

A

Alcyoneus, 22
ancient beliefs, 11, 12
asteroids, 29
astronauts, 42, 43
astronomers, *see* scientists

B

Bell Laboratories, New Jersey, 16
black holes, 22

C

comets, 29

D

dwarf planets, 29

E

Earth, 9, 11, 15, 16, 29, 37, 38
elliptical galaxies, 9

G

galaxy clusters, 25
Galilei, Galileo, 12
gas giants, 34, 37
gases, 30, 34
gravity, 6, 22, 25, 26, 30

H

HAT-P-67b, 37
Hercules-Corona Borealis Great Wall, 25

I

International Space Station (ISS), 41, 42, 43
irregular galaxies, 9

J

Jansky, Karl Guthe, 16
Jupiter, 34, 37, 38

K

Kelly, Scott, 43

L

lenticular galaxy, 9
light, 6, 16, 22
light-years, 6, 25, 29, 37, 38

M

mass, 37, 38
Milky Way, 9, 11, 12, 15
moons, 26, 29, 34

O

orbiting, 26, 29, 34

P

planets, 4, 6, 26, 29, 34, 37, 38, 44

R

radio astronomy, 16, 18, 21
radio telescopes, 18, 21
radio waves, 16, 18
red hypergiant stars, 32
rockets, 41
rocks, 6
rovers, 41
ROXs 42 B b, 38

S

satellites, 41
scientists, 6, 12, 15, 16, 18, 22, 25, 37, 44
shapes, 9, 30
solar system, 29, 34, 37
spiral galaxies, 9
star systems, 4, 6, 16, 26, 29, 30, 34
stars, 4, 6, 9, 12, 26, 29, 30, 32, 34, 44
sun, 9, 29, 30, 32
superclusters, 25

T

telescopes, 12, 15, 16, 18, 21, 41

U

universe, 4, 44
UY Scuti, 32

Y

yellow dwarf stars, 32